MW01591462

An Operational Reserve for New Domains

Designing a Selected Reserve Augmentee System for the 21st Century

STEPHEN DALZELL, DANIEL B. GINSBERG, JONATHAN WELCH,
RYAN HABERMAN

Prepared for the United States Space Command
Approved for public release; distribution is unlimited.

 NATIONAL SECURITY RESEARCH DIVISION

For more information on this publication, visit **www.rand.org/t/RRA1855-1**.

About RAND

RAND is a research organization that develops solutions to public policy challenges to help make communities throughout the world safer and more secure, healthier and more prosperous. RAND is nonprofit, nonpartisan, and committed to the public interest. To learn more about RAND, visit www.rand.org.

Research Integrity

Our mission to help improve policy and decisionmaking through research and analysis is enabled through our core values of quality and objectivity and our unwavering commitment to the highest level of integrity and ethical behavior. To help ensure our research and analysis are rigorous, objective, and nonpartisan, we subject our research publications to a robust and exacting quality-assurance process; avoid both the appearance and reality of financial and other conflicts of interest through staff training, project screening, and a policy of mandatory disclosure; and pursue transparency in our research engagements through our commitment to the open publication of our research findings and recommendations, disclosure of the source of funding of published research, and policies to ensure intellectual independence. For more information, visit www.rand.org/about/research-integrity.

RAND's publications do not necessarily reflect the opinions of its research clients and sponsors.

Published by the RAND Corporation, Santa Monica, Calif.
© 2025 RAND Corporation
RAND® is a registered trademark.

Library of Congress Cataloging-in-Publication Data is available for this publication.

ISBN: 978-1-9774-1336-9

Cover: John Ayre/U.S. Space Command.

About This Report

In this report, we compare the U.S. Space Command's (USSPACECOM'S) assigned missions and responsibilities and the potential contributions from reserve component (RC) personnel, and we examine the systems currently in place to document RC requirements, source individual reserve members from the services, and access and activate these individuals when needed.

This project began in November 2021, and unpublished findings specific to USSPACECOM requirements were provided to the command separately in 2024.

The research reported here was completed in May 2024 and underwent security review with the sponsor and the Defense Office of Prepublication and Security Review before public release.

RAND National Security Research Division

This research was sponsored by USSPACECOM and conducted within the Personnel, Readiness, and Health (PRH) Program of the RAND National Security Research Division (NSRD), which operates the National Defense Research Institute (NDRI), a federally funded research and development center sponsored by the Office of the Secretary of Defense, the Joint Staff, the Unified Combatant Commands, the Navy, the Marine Corps, the defense agencies, and the defense intelligence enterprise.

For more information on the RAND Personnel, Readiness, and Health Program, see www.rand.org/nsrd/prh or contact the director (contact information is provided on the webpage).

Acknowledgments

This research benefited from the support and expertise offered by a succession of USSPACECOM staff members in two key offices: Col Agustin Carrero, Col Lisa Johnson, CDR Andrew Schaaf, and MAJ Holly Kellmurray of the Reserve Component Forces and Manpower Directorate (J014) and Amy Washburn and LtCol John Ball of the Human Capital Directorate (J1). Molly McIntosh, PRH Program Director, gave us firm leadership and encouragement throughout the course of this project. We also benefited greatly from the knowledge and wisdom of RAND colleagues who are also working in the military space field, including Lisa Harrington and RAND Space Enterprise Initiative Lead Bruce McClintock, and our internal reviewer, Al Robbert.

Summary

To execute its mission, the U.S. Space Command (USSPACECOM) requires highly capable individuals and, like any other large organization, must deal with ebbs and flows in its labor demand. One short- to medium-term solution to maintaining a capable force is to employ service members from the highly skilled reserve components (RCs) of the military services.

USSPACECOM engaged the RAND National Defense Research Institute to review legislation, policies, and processes for RC requirements and to identify the challenges to fully leveraging this support. In addition to a legal, policy, and process review, we carried out interviews with leaders and subject-matter experts within USSPACECOM and other combatant commands (CCMDs), service representatives, and officials who have responsibility for reserve matters within the Office of the Secretary of Defense.

Key Findings

Our analysis resulted in the following findings:

- Both the manpower requirements systems and processes and the policies and procedures for accessing and activating personnel often reflect outdated assumptions about RC utilization.
- The U.S. Department of Defense's process for utilizing reserve personnel is not optimized for CCMDs to take full advantage of RC capabilities.
- A revised approach to accessing reserve personnel would start with the principles that (1) RC requirements based on plans for warfighting are not inherently more valid than those for other CCMD missions and (2) priority should be given to requirements that support a command's accomplishment of enduring missions directed by higher authorities.

Recommendations

To implement these principles, we recommend the following policy changes:

- The Office of the Secretary of Defense should clarify that valid Selected Reserve augmentee (SRA) requirements might be present across the spectrum of conflict, not just for large-scale combat operations or other scenarios for major RC mobilization. Senior leaders should reinforce the SRA program with strategic communication.
- USSPACECOM should work with the military departments and the Joint Staff to ensure that the requirements process takes into account mission areas short of mobilization, including operations other than war, contingency operations, and missions requiring skills and specialties found in the RC.

- CCMDs should pursue clarification and expansion of the available activation authorities, such as the authority for preplanned mobilization, to support utilization of SRA personnel for operational mission areas.
- The services and CCMDs should examine budgets (i.e., funding allocations for exercise support or utilization of mobilization authorities) to ensure that adequate funding is available when the requirements and authorities—including the ability to pay for reserve personnel with service operations and maintenance funds—are in place to use SRAs across the range of operational requirements.

Contents

Tables

An Operational Reserve for New Domains: Designing a Selected Reserve Augmentee System for the 21st Century

The U.S. Space Command (USSPACECOM) states its mission as follows: "U.S. Space Command, working with Allies and Partners, plans, executes, and integrates military spacepower into multi-domain global operations in order to deter aggression, defend national interests, and when necessary, defeat threats.[1]" This lofty mission is executed by service members from across the joint force, civilians, and contractors. To execute this mission, USSPACECOM requires highly capable individuals and, like any other large organization, must deal with ebbs and flows in its labor demand. One short- to medium-term solution to maintaining a capable force is to employ service members from the highly skilled reserve components (RCs) of the military services. RC service members can also help provide continuity by covering staffing gaps and turnover and provide unique technical skillsets that are unrepresented or underrepresented in the active component. However, even when there are capable and available volunteers, challenges remain for defining, validating, sourcing, and assigning reservists to support the mission.

Combatant commands (CCMDs) utilize personnel from the RCs in numerous ways. Individuals can be ordered to active duty as full-time support duty, often referred to as *Active Guard Reserve* or *Training and Administration of the Reserves*, based on U.S. Code, Title 10, Section 12310.[2] At the other end of the spectrum, RC personnel who have no connection to the CCMD can be mobilized in wartime and assigned to fill requests for forces for a specific contingency. In this report, we focus on the middle ground: RC members assigned in peacetime to positions that are aligned to expected operational requirements at the CCMD. These RC personnel are commonly referred to as *Individual Mobilization Augmentees* (IMAs), but neither that term nor its generally understood characteristics are fully appropriate to the questions we are posing.

---

[1] U.S. Space Command (USSPACECOM), homepage, undated-b.

[2] MyNavy HR, "Training and Administration of the Reserves (TAR)," webpage, undated; U.S. Code, Title 10, Armed Forces; Subtitle E, Reserve Components; Part II, Personnel Generally; Chapter 1209, Active Duty; Section 12301, Reserve Components Generally. Paragraph (a)(1) of U.S. Code, Title 10, Section 12310, specifies that the purpose of these assignments is for "organizing, administering, recruiting, instructing, or training the reserve components," but the services have generally been given considerable latitude in how this is interpreted (U.S. Code, Title 10, Armed Forces; Subtitle E, Reserve Components; Part II, Personnel Generally; Chapter 1209, Active Duty; Section 12310, Reserves: For Organizing, Administering, Etc., Reserve Components).

For that reason, we will use the term *Selected Reserve augmentee* (SRA) for the focus of this study. SRA personnel might be directly assigned to the supported command (as with IMAs), or to an administrative unit (such as the supported command's Army Reserve Element). For the purposes of this report, administrative units are distinct from RC operational units because they are not designed to be mobilized as a unit but to provide an RC unit to which personnel can be assigned and that works with the combatant command to ensure that those personnel meet documented readiness requirements for duty on the CCMD staff (e.g., personnel evaluations, medical readiness, fitness tests).

USSPACECOM engaged the RAND National Defense Research Institute to review legislation, policies, and processes for RC requirements and to identify the challenges to fully leveraging this support. In addition to a legal, policy, and process review, we carried out interviews between January and June 2022 and between January and March 2024 with leaders and subject-matter experts within USSPACECOM and other CCMDs,[3] service representatives, and officials who have responsibility for reserve matters within the Office of the Secretary of Defense.

In this report, we divide the utilization of RC manpower into three general phases: (1) defining and validating requirements, (2) sourcing and assigning personnel, and (3) accessing personnel (i.e., calling them to a period of active duty and identifying a funding mechanism). For each of these three phases, we describe the current system, identify problems or challenges within the status quo, and offer potential solutions. Before discussing each phase, we first explore why reserve component personnel are appropriate for CCMD positions, the demand for these personnel generally in nontraditional commands, and SRA support to USSPACECOM more specifically.

One critical caveat is that the newest service, the United States Space Force (USSF), is attempting a radical shift from the personnel models of its predecessors. Under the Space Force Personnel Management Act, part of the 2024 National Defense Authorization Act, there will be no USSF RC, just guardians serving "not on sustained duty" (equivalent to the Selected Reserve) or on inactive duty (the Individual Ready Reserve counterpart).[4] However, we believe that, for the immediate future, CCMDs requesting guardians to meet either full- or part-time requirements will need to validate these requirements using the existing processes. How the USSF will manage the commitments of these individuals to units that do not use the USSF's own flexible scheduling system remains to be seen.

Why Assign RC Personnel to CCMD Positions?

The U.S. Department of Defense (DoD) derives the entire area of RC management from statutes on military reserves to meet command needs.[5] U.S. Code Title 10 provides for the ability to have

---

[3] These were the U.S. Transportation Command, the U.S. Cyber Command, the U.S. Northern Command, and the U.S. Strategic Command.

[4] Thomas Novelly, "Space Force Guardians Can Now Choose to Work Part Time Under New Policy Change," military.com, January 18, 2024.

[5] Section 3819 of Title 50, for example, provides authority for the President to order reserve members and units to active service and release them from duty (U.S. Code, Title 50, War and National Defense; Chapter 49, Military Selective Service; Section 3819, Authority of President to Order Reserve Components to Active Service; Release from Active Duty; Retention of Unit Organizations and Equipment).

reserve billets and to fill those billets with trained personnel.[6] Unlike the full-time support program, for example, there is nothing in Title 10 that establishes IMAs as a separate duty status or delineates their purpose, nor is there a statutory requirement for IMAs and other part-time personnel types to have a certain number of annual training days beyond the baseline training prescribed in Title 10, Section 10147, or meet a particular type of requirement. Therefore, DoD has wide latitude to tailor these programs to best meet CCMD requirements.

DoD has laid out its policy for utilization of IMAs—whether in a CCMD or another component—in DoD Instruction (DoDI) 1235.11, *Management of Individual Mobilization Augmentees*.[7] The instruction sets basic policies, divides responsibilities among responsible organizations, and sets forth management processes and procedures. Numerous other DoD policies that govern aspects of SRA utilization, including utilization of reserve intelligence personnel, will be discussed later.[8]

During steady state operations, there are several reasons why it is useful to employ reservists, most of which are codified in DoDI 1235.11. The policy explicitly states that

> Individual Reserve Component (RC) military billets that augment the Active Component (AC) structure of the DoD or other departments or agencies of the U.S. Government and must be filled to support **mobilization requirements, contingency operations, operations other than war, or other specialized or technical requirements** may be validated for fill with IMA members of the Selected Reserve.[9]

The leaders and subject-matter experts interviewed during this study said that SRA members perform at a higher level than reserve members brought in without previous affiliation. Assigned members have already spent the necessary time to inprocess and onboard at the unit and know their way around the command both physically and organizationally. Often, individual augmentees are already trained and understand key business processes, decision chains, and standard operating procedures. In more practical terms, they should have current clearances, read-ins, badges, and systems access. As a result, an individual augmentee can have an immediate impact and operate at a higher level, according to our interviewees. Interviewees also pointed out how SRAs can provide continuity, especially when occupants of key billets are out of the office or when there is a delay before replacements are identified. Additionally, in the case of USSPACECOM, which has such a highly specialized and technical mission set, accessing experts who work on a related matter in their civilian job can be particularly helpful.

---

[6] U.S. Code, Title 10, Armed Forces; Subtitle E, Reserve Components; Part I, Organization and Administration; Chapter 1005, Elements of Reserve Components; Section 10142, Ready Reserve: Selected Reserve.

[7] DoDI 1235.11, *Management of Individual Mobilization Augmentees (IMAs)*, Under Secretary of Defense for Personnel and Readiness, July 10, 2015.

[8] For example, DoDI 1205.18 governs the full-time support program, which SRAs can fall under after activation, and DoDI 3325.11 provides policies on reserve integration into intelligence matters (DoDI 1205.18, *Full-Time Support (FTS) to the Reserve Components*, Office of the Under Secretary of Defense for Personnel and Readiness, June 5, 2020; DoDI 3325.11, *Management of the Joint Reserve Intelligence Program (JRIP)*, Under Secretary of Defense for Intelligence and Security, June 26, 2015, change 2, September 24, 2020).

[9] DoDI 1235.11, 2015, p. 1, emphasis added.

Nature of Demand for Part-Time Manpower at a Nontraditional CCMD

All three phases of RC manpower utilization—defining and validating requirements, sourcing and assigning personnel, and accessing personnel—include some consideration of the requirements generated by CCMDs and other headquarters. But what is the nature of those demands, particularly for nontraditional CCMDs?

Evolving Expectations of Reserve Component Roles

We interpret the current language in Chairman of the Joint Chiefs of Staff Instruction (CJCSI) 1001.01C as reflecting the period in which the IMA program and other RC programs originated, when RC manpower assigned to the CCMDs was viewed as a strategic reserve.[10] RC member service in annual training and, in some cases, inactive duty for training was primarily to prepare them for their roles on mobilization. Mobilization would be used only for situations in which a Presidential Selected Reserve Call-Up or higher level of mobilization would be declared and initiated. Throughout the Cold War and the first post–Cold War decade, this assumption about the RC as a strategic reserve was correct.

In the past two decades, however, assumptions about RC utilization have changed; the RC is increasingly employed in more-operational assignments. Although the most visible face of the operational reserve has been in the mobilization of RC units to fill in rotational missions and serve alongside active component units, those assigned to IMA positions or who are available through individual augmentation orders have helped keep higher-level staffs functioning, according to interviewees. Not all these positions would have met the exacting requirements for wartime augmentation as envisioned in CJCSI 1001.01C but nonetheless were needed for the CCMDs to meet a range of requirements.

Moreover, there has been a shift away from interstate combat as the sole focus of military planning, and, with the expansion of national strategy to cover competition and crisis, nonwartime requirements could also be considered adequate justification for RC support. For example, if a robust series of multinational exercises are a critical element of competition in a combatant commander's area of responsibility, it would be as logical to request RC personnel to conduct these exercises as it would be in a much less likely war against a rival power.

Because USSPACECOM is responsible for a physical space—an "astrographic area of responsibility" beginning 100 kilometers above mean sea level[11]—DoD classifies it as a geographic combatant command. However, in terms of missions and personnel requirements, we feel USSPACECOM is more similar to functional commands such as U.S. Cyber Command and U.S. Strategic Command. Instead of lengthy build-up periods as countries mobilize forces followed by a defined period of conventional, kinetic battle, these newer commands can experience repeated spikes in activity because of global events and periods when requests for support come from different

---

[10] CJCSI 1001.01C, *Joint Manpower and Personnel Program*, Joint Chiefs of Staff, February 21, 2024.

[11] U.S. Space Command, "Frequently Asked Questions," webpage, undated-a.

geographic CCMDs in response to events in their associated countries and international waters. To avoid misusing the doctrinal terms, this report uses *nontraditional combatant command* when distinguishing the latter from those commands focused on areas of the earth's surface. As we describe later, a simple review of the missions explicitly given to USSPACECOM in the Unified Command Plan (UCP) reveals how much of its role lies outside wartime tasks. Constraining access to RC support seems to reflect an outdated notion of what constitutes strategic activities, at these nontraditional CCMDs in particular.

Finally, seeing RC augmentees primarily as a supplementary force for active component capabilities is at odds with the services' own evolving conceptions of their RCs. To varying degrees, the services are talking more than ever about the way individuals from their RCs can bring specialized civilian skills or military skills that a unit does not need for daily activities.[12] These are not necessarily wartime requirements but instead might present as cyclical demands even in peacetime. In the first phase of this process, examples of useful civilian skills mentioned by subject-matter experts interviewed for this study included using data for process management (from an interviewee who has a career in civilian industry), sensor management (from a DoD civilian working in missile defense), and artificial intelligence (from a corporate information technology director). Using RC personnel to meet these variable requirements can conserve full-time authorizations for more-continuous tasks, offering an efficient way for the DoD enterprise to meet the mission.

SRA Support to Specific USSPACECOM Mission Requirements

Not all CCMD mission requirements are created equal. Some mission sets might be a better fit for SRA support, whereas others might be best suited for active-component personnel, given those individuals are embedded within the CCMD full-time, and still other mission sets can be supported by RC personnel coming from the Individual Ready Reserve or other parts of the Selected Reserve for one-time duty. To assess requirements suitable for RC personnel, we first sought to understand the different types of mission requirements tasked to all CCMDs and the specific responsibilities outlined for USSPACECOM in particular.

The UCP is a DoD document, signed by the President, outlining mission requirements that all CCMDs must perform and specific responsibilities tasked to particular CCMDs.[13] The UCP is updated roughly every two years to reflect changes in national security and defense priorities along with changes in the global threat environment. We reviewed three recent UCPs (from 2017, 2020, and 2022) and extracted mission requirements and responsibilities that all CCMDs are tasked to conduct—with those outlined for USSPACECOM of particular interest. Table 1 shows some of the specific responsibilities assigned to each CCMD in the 2022 UCP. Although most CCMDs have at least one responsibility that goes beyond combat operations, nontraditional commands tend to have more non-combat responsibilities than geographic CCMDs have. Our aim is to understand

---

[12] Reserve Forces Policy Board, *Improving the Total Force: Using the National Guard and Reserves*, RFPB Report FY20-01, August 14, 2020.

[13] The 2020 and 2022 UCP documents are overall classified as controlled unclassified information (CUI); however, all material relevant to our analysis is at the unclassified level.

USSPACECOM's explicitly directed missions and assess which of these might be a good fit for support from SRAs.

Table 1. CCMD UCP-Specific Responsibilities, 2022

Type	Command	Count of Specific Responsibilities	Specific Responsibilities
Geographic	U.S. Africa Command	None	n/a
Geographic	U.S. Central Command	None	n/a
Functional	U.S. Cyber Command	3	Cyberspace operations, cyberspace operations joint force provider, trainer for DoD Cyberspace Operations Forces
Geographic	U.S. European Command	1	Commander, U.S. European Command, normally designated Supreme Allied Commander Europe
Geographic	U.S. Indo-Pacific Command	4	Homeland defense, support to civil authorities, missions in the Russian Federation, advocating for required capabilities in the area of responsibility
Geographic	U.S. Northern Command	8	Homeland defense; Commander of North American Aerospace Defense Command; Commander, U.S. Element of the North American Aerospace Defense Command; Arctic issues; support to civil authorities; chemical, biological, radiological, and nuclear response; pandemic influenza and infectious diseases; point of contact for military matters in its area of responsibility
Geographic	U.S. Southern Command	1	Defense of the Panama Canal and Panama Canal area
Geographic	U.S. Space Command	5	Space operations (including DoD manager for human space flight and provision of capabilities, such as environmental monitoring; surveillance and reconnaissance; and positioning, navigation, and timing [PNT]); global sensing manager; global satellite communications operations; trans-regional missile defense (TRMD); space operations joint force provider
Functional	U.S. Special Operations Command	5	Global special operations forces operations, special operations forces joint force provider, joint special operations forces training, countering violent extremist organizations and other threat networks, countering weapons of mass destruction
Functional	U.S. Strategic Command	6	Strategic deterrence; nuclear operations; nuclear command, control, and communications; joint electromagnetic spectrum operations; global strike; missile threat assessment
Functional	U.S. Transportation Command	6	Mobility joint orce provider, DoD single manager for transportation, joint deployment and distribution enterprise, DoD single manager for patient movement, joint-enabling capabilities, DoD single manager for global bulk fuel management and delivery

SOURCE: Features information from DoD, *2022 Unified Command Plan*, April 25, 2023, Not available to the general public.
NOTE: n/a = not applicable.

There might be a most favorable context for use of SRAs that can be defined by three dimensions: scale, lead time, and duration. We are speaking here of missions as occasions when the command is actively fulfilling a particular responsibility. As an analogy, although U.S. Southern Command is always responsible for defending the Panama Canal, we would be looking for those instances in which it needs additional personnel to conduct an exercise or plan a show of force to achieve that end. On the one extreme, missions with a large scale or long lead time or duration are well-suited for being filled through the regular global force management allocation process with active component personnel or units, or with reservists from other units who can be trained and onboarded for the mission. On the other extreme, requirements with a short lead time or duration could arise and end too quickly to activate an RC individual, even one aligned to the position. Missions of medium scale, lead time, and duration would be the best fit for SRA support.

We then analyzed each of USSPACECOM's assigned responsibilities against these dimensions using the following definitions:

- *Scale* is the number of individuals needed to complete the requirement, broken into large (L, 50 or more personnel), medium (M, 11 to 49 personnel), and small (S, 10 or fewer personnel).
- *Lead time* is how far in advance of a requirement the command knew about it, broken into long (L, six months to one year), medium (M, two weeks to six months), and short (S, less than two weeks).
- *Duration* is the average length of time augmentees would be required for the mission, broken into long (L, greater than one year), medium (M, three months to one year), and short (S, less than three months).

We shared our assessment with USSPACECOM and modified our scores when the command provided additional data about how it would meet surge requirements for some of the missions. When directorates differed in their assessments, we used the score that would best justify use of SRAs, because we are looking for cases in which any tasks could be done by reservists, not in which *every* directorate needed augmentees. Table 2 shows the results. We determined that SRA personnel might be well-suited for missions with small to medium scale, medium lead time, and medium duration.

Using this framework, results from subject-matter expert inputs at USSPACECOM's joint directorates reveal a few high-level missions that would be a perfect fit to incorporate SRA personnel. Three of USSPACECOM's main missions were adjudicated as being large in scale, having a long lead time, and having a long duration: space operations, being DoD's global sensing manager, and being DoD's global satellite communications operations manager. Although this adjudication places these missions outside the scope for what we hypothesize as being the optimal situation for SRA support, it does not rule out part-time support for the mission set. Some of these tasks might not be performed at the headquarters level and are instead managed by the service component, where active duty or reserve component personnel could both equally support.

Table 2. Assessment of USSPACECOM UCP Responsibilities

Responsibility	Scale	Lead Time	Duration
Space operations			
Plan and execute global space operations	L	L	L
Conduct offensive and defensive space operations	L	M	L
Protect and defend U.S. and allies' and partners' commercial space operational capabilities	L	M	M
Advocate for space operations capabilities	M	M	S
Serve as DoD manager for human space flight operations	L	L	L
Provide warning and assessment of attack on space assets, defend orbit space assets and data links, and coordinate with other CCMDs for defense of USSPACECOM terrestrial assets	M	S	M
Provide space capabilities, such as satellite communications; missile warning; nuclear detonation detection; environmental monitoring; military intelligence, surveillance, and reconnaissance; and PNT for CCMDs, allies, and partners	L	L	L
Global sensing manager			
Plan, manage, and conduct operations of assigned DoD space domain awareness, missile defense and missile warning sensors, trans-regional networks, and associated command and control networks	L	L	L
Synchronize, integrate, and provide operational sensor data to other CCMDs, U.S. agencies, and others as directed	L	L	L
Global satellite communications operations			
Plan, manage, allocate, adjudicate, and execute DoD satellite communications (narrowband, wideband, protected, and leased commercial) in support of other CCMDs and other entities	L	L	L
TRMD			
Conduct TRMD planning and operations support in coordination with other CCMDs; the services; and, as directed, appropriate U.S. government agencies, allies, and partners	S	M	M
Support assessment of missile defense operational capabilities	S	S	L
Ensure continuity of operations in trans-regional missile defense operations	S	M	M
Space operations joint force provider			
Identify and recommend global joint sourcing solutions to the chairman of the Joint Chiefs of Staff in coordination with the services and other CCMDs and supervise the implementation of sourcing decisions	S	L	M

SOURCE: Features information from DoD, 2023 and subject-matter experts, interviews with the authors.

In other cases, joint directorates' input were at odds with one another, suggesting that each directorate might have separate requirements for utilizing part-time support for high-level missions. One example of this was USSPACECOM's responsibility to be the space joint force provider. An operations directorate indicated this mission as small in scale, long in lead time, and long in duration. The plans directorate noted this as small in scale, short in lead time, and short in duration. The training directorate also diverged, indicating the mission to be small in scale, long in lead time, and medium in duration.

One mission did stand out, however, as fitting our criteria for a most favorable scenario for SRA personnel: USSPACECOM's mission to conduct trans-regional missile defense planning and operations support. Agreement among directorates and our analysis indicated it as small in scale, medium in lead time, and medium in duration.

This analysis highlighted mission sets within the UCP that are particularly well-suited for SRAs to support. To leverage that support and bring SRA personnel to bear to their full potential, it is necessary to assess the system for formally defining and validating SRA manpower requirements, sourcing and assigning SRA personnel, and accessing those forces. In each of these areas—requirements, sourcing, and accessing—we review the current state, issues, and potential solutions in the sections that follow.

Defining and Validating Requirements

To employ RC service members, CCMDs must first define and validate their requirements. In accordance with DoDI 1235.11, "IMAs are assigned against validated RC billets that are identified on [active component] force structure documents for fill by RC members."[14] This instruction also outlines the assignment, training, and requirements for IMAs. The formal requirements and validation process, for all joint personnel, is described in detail in CJCSI 1001.01C.[15]

The Joint Manpower Program seeks to "ensure that joint activities have the minimum manpower with the appropriate skills and experience to carry out assigned missions, tasks, and functions."[16] CJCSI 1001.01C directs combatant commanders to "[e]stablish internal policies and procedures for determining, validating, documenting, and prioritizing joint manpower requirements that comply with DoD and [Chairman, Joint Chiefs of Staff] guidelines" and review their Joint Manpower Program annually.[17] Any desired changes are submitted to the Joint Staff as part of the Joint Manpower Program process, which is composed of a continual five-step cycle:

1. analysis of organization's mission and external taskings
2. determination of manpower requirements
3. validation and resourcing of requirements
4. documentation of funded requirements

---

[14] DoDI 1235.11, 2015, p. 1.

[15] CJCSI 1001.01C, 2024, Enclosure B.

[16] CJCSI 1001.01C, 2024, Enclosure B, p. B-1.

[17] CJCSI 1001.01C, 2024, Enclosure A, p. A-2.

5. review and updating of requirements.[18]

The first two steps are conducted by the CCMD and can take as much time as needed for thorough analysis (the size of the gap between the current and proposed structures being the key variable in how long is needed). Any requests for new manpower must go through the Joint Manpower Validation Process, which involves a review by the Operations Deputies Tank. If approved, the request continues to the Joint Manning Validation Board, where, if approved again, it results in a change in the Joint Table of Distribution or the Joint Table of Mobilization Distribution (JTMD).[19]

Determining RC requirements for the JTMD is particularly complicated because the process builds on the validated full-time structure and other factors. The CJCSI essentially lays out three steps for determining requirements for SRAs:

1. Determine total wartime workload (to include continuous peacetime missions).
2. Assume all active component and civilian personnel will work 60 hours per week.
3. Identify what additional workload remains and request selected reserve support to cover the balance.[20]

The current system faces a few considerable challenges. First, according to interviewees, it can be difficult to forecast the number of hours required during wartime or a contingency. Part of the math is simply calculating the manpower for sustained 24-hour operations, but other knowledge-work functions, such as planning, can be extremely unpredictable.[21] Second, the experts interviewed for this study said that it is hard to define *wartime*, especially as it relates to the space domain. Against the backdrop of competition, the dual-use nature of many space systems and the heavy reliance on them for a variety of functions can lead to a disproportionately greater demand for space operations than what might be seen in other domains or experienced by other CCMDs. The closest analogy is likely cyberspace.[22]

Finally, there seems to be a misalignment of policy with instructions and the resulting processes. As explained earlier, DoDI 1235.11 states that it is DoD policy that members in RC positions that augment the active component can be used for four general purposes: mobilization requirements, contingency operations, operations other than war, and other specialized or technical requirements.[23]

Nearly identical language is used in CJCSI 1001.01C, which guides the Joint Manpower and Personnel Program:

> IMA authorizations are individual military manpower positions identified as
> necessary to augment the Active Component (AC) structure of the Department of

---

[18] CJCSI 1001.01C, 2024, Enclosure B.

[19] CJCSI 1001.01C, 2024, Enclosure B. CJCSI 1001.01C, Enclosure J, "Joint Mobilization Requirements and Reserve Support to Joint Activities," specifies that Selected Reserve (IMA) requirements are documented on the JTMD, whereas Active Guard Reserve and Full-Time Support requirements are documented on the Joint Table of Distribution (CJCSI 1001.01C, 2024, Enclosure J).

[20] CJCSI 1001.01C, 2024, Enclosure J.

[21] Subject-matter experts, interviews with the authors.

[22] Subject-matter experts, interviews with the authors.

[23] DoDI 1235.11, 2015, p. 1.

Defense or other U.S. Government departments or agencies *to support mobilization (including premobilization and/or post-mobilization) requirements, contingency operations, operations other than war, or other specialized or technical requirements.*[24]

However, one page later, the instruction uses distinctly different language when describing how joint commands should actually calculate their Selective Reserve requirements: "Joint activities should determine and document their total wartime workload, including all wartime missions and peacetime missions that continue during a war or contingency."[25] On the same page, the instruction states, "The JTMD identifies the additional manpower and organization required to shift to a wartime, contingency, or mobilization footing."[26] The first two quotations imply a distinction between contingencies and operations other than war. A *contingency* is defined by DoD as a "situation requiring military operations in response to natural disasters, terrorists, subversives, or as otherwise directed by appropriate authority to protect US interests."[27] The term *operations other than war* was removed from the official DoD lexicon in April 2001,[28] but while in use it encompassed a broader set of activities, including "noncombatant evacuation operations, disaster relief, humanitarian assistance, peacekeeping, peace enforcement, counterterrorism, and counternarcotics," as described in a 1995 RAND report.[29]

Although one might debate the distinctions between a contingency and an operation other than war, we believe that the more important feature is the exclusion in both cases of "specialized or technical requirements." Logically, this would prevent a joint command from building augmentee positions with the intent of leveraging RC personnel based on civilian-acquired space industry skills, for example, to efficiently meet missions outside real-world operations. In our interviews with members of the Joint Staff and others involved in the process, this more restrictive definition of IMA is the one used to validate CCMD submissions of reserve requirements to the Joint Manning Validation Board.

A solution for addressing the second and third challenges—difficulty in defining warfare as it relates to the space domain and the apparent misalignment of policy and instruction—is broadening the Joint Staff's criteria for SRA position validation to include operations other than war and "other specialized or technical requirements." Simply modifying Enclosure J to use the reasons for using

---

[24] CJCSI 1001.01C, 2024, Enclosure J, p. J-1, emphasis added.

[25] CJCSI 1001.01C, 2024, Enclosure J, p. J-2.

[26] CJCSI 1001.01C, 2024, Enclosure J, p. J-2.

[27] Joint Chiefs of Staff, *DoD Dictionary of Military and Associated Terms*, April 2024, p. 41.

[28] Joint Chiefs of Staff, "DoD Terminology Program," webpage, undated. Although the term is not in the dictionary, a search for it elicits a note that "OOTW has been deleted from the DoD Dictionary. Reason: 04/12/01: Deletion approved in revision of JP 1-02." JP 3-07, which had provided joint doctrine for operations other than war, is now titled *Joint Stabilization Activities*; the *DoD Dictionary* defines *stability activities* as

> [v]arious military missions, tasks, and activities conducted outside the United States in coordination with other instruments of national power to maintain or reestablish a safe and secure environment and provide essential governmental services, emergency infrastructure reconstruction, and humanitarian relief (Joint Chiefs of Staff, 2024, p. 221).

Because the policy documents we are referencing have not been changed to reflect this terminology, and there is a clear difference between them, we will continue to use the older term here.

[29] Taw, Jennifer, and John E. Peters, *Operations Other Than War: Implications for the U.S. Army*, RAND Corporation, MR-566-A, 1995, p. x.

SRAs found in DoDI 1235.11 would make the definition of wartime moot and resolve the mismatched language in the policy documents. However, the first challenge—estimating the workload associated with wartime or a contingency—cannot be alleviated. It is a challenge faced by all CCMDs, and it is a particularly tough challenge for a new command with an evolving mission.

Sourcing and Assigning RC Personnel

In the second phase in this process, the services source personnel to fill validated requirements (i.e., accept responsibility to identify, assign, and manage individual service members for each position). In theory, requirements are service-agnostic—the supported command is supposed to say it needs an imagery intelligence specialist in the grade of E-6, for example, not that it needs an Army 35G (Geospatial Intelligence Imagery Analyst). Here we are distinguishing between personnel put on permanent orders that assign them to a unit and those put on temporary orders that direct them to report for active duty to complete a discrete task, such as supporting an exercise or filling in for a missing active component service member.

In our interviews, we did not find systematic problems associated with sourcing and assignment of personnel. Clearly, every joint headquarters would prefer that each validated position has a trained and consistently ready incumbent, and few are fully satisfied on that score.[30] From our experiences with other commands, USSPACECOM's concerns seemed consistent with those expressed elsewhere. Because there are no identified sourcing issues, there is no discussion here on potential solutions.

Accessing RC Personnel

In the third phase in the process, the command takes the necessary actions for calling the assigned RC personnel to duty in response to real-world demand.[31] Utilizing an RC member at a CCMD requires the alignment of three things: (1) a ready, willing, and appropriately skilled individual; (2) the legal authority to call them to active duty for this purpose; and (3) the funding for the individual's pay and allowances, travel, and other costs. In many cases, a memorandum between the CCMD and the relevant service or RC is also required.

DoD components, including commands, typically utilize activated reserve personnel for two fundamental purposes beyond training: providing support for ongoing operations or mobilization for emergencies. Under both conditions, the CCMDs must receive the basic authorization to draw an SRA member away from their civilian lives into active duty. Table 3 lists relevant mobilization authorities. Title 10, Section 12301(d) allows the secretary of a military department to order a member to active duty under a voluntary basis, although Section 12304(b) allows, in some cases, reserve members within established units to be called to duty involuntarily for budgetarily programmed preplanned missions.

---

[30] Subject-matter experts, interviews with the authors.

[31] We are consciously excluding from our discussion how the RC personnel are put on orders for scheduled training (typically for a weekend or two weeks of annual training, although there are other variations) and requesting additional personnel be mobilized and then assigned to the command.

CCMDs can also access SRAs beyond their baseline requirements with a Presidential Declaration under U.S. Code, Title 10, Section 12301(a), which provides for a full-scale mobilization.[32] Section 12302 allows the secretary of the military departments to activate a reserve member for up to 24 months and limits the total number of call-ups to no more than one million at any point,[33] and Section 12304 allows the Secretary of Defense to activate a member for no more than 365 days to support a "named operational mission," limiting the total number activated at one time to no more than 200,000.[34] Interviewees suggested that the two authorities most relevant for accessing reserve members for ongoing mission areas and surges of operations are 12031(a) and 12304, allowing the CCMDs to increase their capacity before hostilities begin.[35]

Table 3. Involuntary Mobilization Authorities

Source	Section	Category
U.S. Code, Title 10	12301(a)	Full mobilization
U.S. Code, Title 10	12302	Partial mobilization
U.S. Code, Title 10	12304	Presidential Reserve Call-Up
U.S. Code, Title 10	12304a	Major disasters or emergencies
U.S. Code, Title 10	12304b	Preplanned CCMD missions
U.S. Code, Title 10	12301(b)	Short periods of active duty (no more than 15 days)
U.S. Code, Title 14	712	Secretary of Homeland Security Coast Guard Reserve call-ups for domestic emergencies
U.S. Code, Title 32	502(f)(1)(A)	Involuntary Full Time National Guard Duty

SOURCE: Features information from DoDI 1215.06, *Uniform Reserve, Training, and Retirement Categories for the Reserve Components*, Under Secretary of Defense for Personnel and Readiness, March 11, 2014, change 2, July 12, 2022.

Once the respective authority is validated, an SRA will receive orders from their service, and associated funding for pay, allowances, and entitlements will be provided by the service. In the case of Section 12301(d), SRAs operating in CCMDs are paid for through the Active Duty Operational Support, Active Component (ADOS-AC) or the ManDay program and associated accounts. These programs are part of the service military budgets. Reserve intelligence personnel, who can often fill

---

[32] U.S. Code, Title 10, Section 12301.

[33] U.S. Code, Title 10, Armed Forces; Subtitle E, Reserve Components; Part II, Personnel Generally; Chapter 1209, Active Duty; Section 12302, Ready Reserve.

[34] U.S. Code, Title 10, Armed Forces; Subtitle E, Reserve Components; Part II, Personnel Generally; Chapter 1209, Active Duty; Section 12304, Selected Reserve and Certain Individual Ready Reserve Members; Order to Active Duty Other Than During War or National Emergency.

[35] Subject-matter experts, interviews with the authors. A state war or national emergency must exist to invoke this mobilization authority.

validated positions with the J-2 directorates of the CCMDs, can be paid for out of National Intelligence Program (NIP) and Military Intelligence Program (MIP) funds through a transfer to the service.[36] Pay, benefits, and allowances for SRA personnel on active duty can come out of Reserve Personnel Appropriation (RPA) when the funding is used for ongoing administration of reserve programs, operational missions assigned to reserve personnel, and training. Although it is primarily designated for training purposes, operational missions can be funded through this account when the mission includes a substantial training component.[37]

Additionally, the Funded Reimbursable Authority allows that funds appropriated

> for operation and maintenance of the Military Departments, Combatant Commands and Defense Agencies shall be available for reimbursement of pay, allowances and other expenses which would otherwise be incurred against appropriations for the National Guard and Reserve when members of the National Guard and Reserve provide intelligence or counterintelligence support.[38]

In other words, USSPACECOM can convert operational funds, which it directly controls, to pay and allowance for RC members, which is service-controlled—but only for intelligence purposes. CCMDs can also pay for reserve intelligence personnel through the MIP and NIP.

Finally, such commands as the U.S. Transportation Command can draw from a working capital fund (in this case, the Transportation Working Capital Fund) to pay for activated reserve personnel.

It is challenging for CCMDs to get the authority to access SRAs beyond the baseline training time. For requirements short of full mobilization, such as periodically surging for brief and unscheduled missions, the CCMDs will be limited to voluntary call-ups under U.S. Code, Title 10, Section 12301(d) and involuntary call-ups through Section 12304. Interviewees suggested that the preplanned mobilizations permitted under 12304(b) would not apply to accessing SRAs, particularly IMAs in this case, because this statute's purpose is for mobilization of units, not individuals.[39] Personnel policy experts interviewed for this study said that relatively simple administrative changes could allow the CCMDs to form a unit that would qualify under the provision.[40] Nevertheless, there is ambiguity and confusion about whether the preplanned mission activation would apply. However, even if the CCMDs could tap into this authority, the planning would have to occur well in advance. The services would have to designate funding in their budgets and include justification for that mission in their budget submissions to Congress.

Funding is the most notable challenge that the CCMDs face in accessing assigned reserve forces. Two worlds of SRA access have emerged as the United States has moved away from two conflicts in

---

[36] Department of Defense Instruction 3300.05, *Reserve Component Intelligence Enterprise (RCIE) Management*, Under Secretary of Defense for Intelligence and Security, July 17, 2013, change 2, August 7, 2020, Enclosure 2.

[37] U.S. House of Representatives, Department of Defense Appropriations Act, 2024, Bill 4365, June 27, 2023; U.S. Code, Title 10, Armed Forces; Subtitle E, Reserve Components; Part I, Organization and Administration, Chapter 1007, Administration of Reserve Components; Section 10211, Policies and Regulations: Participation of Reserve Officers in Preparation and Administration; U.S. Code, Title 10, Section 12310.

[38] Public Law 113-6, Consolidated and Further Continuing Appropriations Act, 2013; Section 8043, March 26, 2013. For specific direction to the secretaries of the military departments on this matter, see DoDI 3300.05, 2020.

[39] Subject-matter experts, interviews with the authors.

[40] Subject-matter experts, interviews with the authors.

Southwest Asia but nevertheless continues to maintain a high state of readiness with ongoing operations. Particular mission areas and bureaus and whole CCMDs can access SRAs readily, although others see dwindling availability of resources. Most CCMDs must rely on the ADOS-AC or Man-Day funding that comes out of service budgets. This funding competes against other requirements during the service budgetary process. CCMD representatives said that funding for the voluntary call-ups authorized under Section 12301(d) has remained steady over recent years.

One step forward would be to reinvigorate the focus on all aspects of the SRA program among key stakeholders, including the CCMDs, the Joint Staff, and the services. Particular attention should be paid to communications about both the importance of these personnel to execute the National Defense Strategy and the sufficiency of resources set aside in service budgets for ADOS-AC and other RC duties beyond the minimum annual training.

Another potential change is to expand the Funded Reimbursable Authority beyond intelligence support to other functions of a CCMD staff. The current Chief, Army Reserve, Lieutenant General, Jody Daniels, explicitly asked for such a change in testimony before the House Appropriations Committee in 2024, highlighting cyberspace and information operations as particular functions where the Army Reserve could contribute to current operations.[41] As noted earlier, many of USSPACECOM's assigned missions involve potential workload surges that are well-suited for SRA support. In the past, a command's intelligence directorate might have been the paradigmatic example of such irregular surges, but, at USSPACECOM, the entire command might need to respond in this fashion.

Recommendations

We suggest that a revised system for accessing SRAs start with the following principles in mind:

- Priority should be given to requirements that can be shown to support the command's accomplishment of enduring missions in the UCP, Joint Strategic Capabilities Plan, or other strategy documents approved by the Secretary of Defense or the President.
- RC requirements based on plans for warfighting are not inherently more valid than those for other CCMD missions.
- RC requirements do not have to mirror active component or DoD civilian requirements if they are intended to provide low-density or hard-to-maintain skills more efficiently than the use of full-time billets.
- RC requirements do not need to have a utilization plan that is based on mobilization of the individuals. If the requirement meets all other criteria, the RC utilization plan may be based on a combination of inactive duty training, annual training, active duty for operational support, and other duty statuses.

To implement these principles, we recommend DoD consider the following four primary policy changes.

---

[41] Forbes Breaking News, "National Guard and Military Reserve Leaders Testify Before House Appropriations Committee," video, April 30, 2024.

Reinvigorate Utilization of Selected Reserve Augmentees

Given the important role that SRAs can play in CCMDs, USSPACECOM and the other nontraditional CCMDs should consider reinvigorating the SRA program, working with the Joint Staff and the services to ensure that DoD is fully leveraging its skills and capabilities. In addition to recommendations to reexamine the requirements processes and criteria, call-up authorities, and funding, as discussed in the final recommendation, this reinvigoration should involve high-level communications from the chairman, combatant commanders, and the leaders of the RCs, as well as discussions about SRAs and planning conferences, such as the U.S. Air Force's CORONA senior leader conference. RC leaders cannot be the only stakeholders highlighting the importance of SRAs to the CCMDs.

Review the Requirements Process and Criteria

Given the finite pool of RC personnel, the limited number of authorizations available, and the competing demands among CCMDs and other customers, a centralized and transparent process for validating requirements is necessary. USSPACECOM should work with the military departments and the Joint Staff to ensure that the requirements process accounts for mission areas short of mobilization, including operations other than war, contingency operations, and other specialty requirements. This process would begin by modifying CJCSI 1001.01C, Enclosure J, to include all the reasons for using SRAs found in DoDI 1235.11. Moreover, the UCP analysis summarized in this report highlights several missions that would be ideal for SRA support, particularly with advanced civilian skills in cyber, space-systems maintenance and management, risk analysis, international relations, and operations research.

Clarify and Pursue Activation Authorities

The CCMDs generally have sufficient authorities to activate and access their assigned part-time reservists, whether through U.S. Code, Title 10, Section 12301(d) or a Presidential Reserve Call-Up. The CCMDs should further pursue activations of U.S. Code, Title 10, Section 12304(b), preplanned mission authority, to provide an additional avenue for accessing SRAs. Moreover, the services should cooperate with the Joint Staff and provide the CCMDs with guidance on how to ensure that the processes for requesting SRAs comply with the vision for the authority to apply to units.

Expand SRA Funding Models

The services, in conjunction with the CCMDs, should examine budgets to ensure adequate funding when the requirements and authorities are in place. The utilization of reserve intelligence personnel—whereby the services are reimbursed through the NIP and MIP, along with the authority to pay for reserve personnel with service operations and maintenance funds—provides an example of how to create a more robust and vibrant full-time program. Consideration should also be given to clarifying and expanding the use of RPA to include SRA augmentation of the active force.

Abbreviations

ADOS-AC	Active Duty Operational Support, Active Component
CCMD	combatant command
CJCSI	Chairman of the Joint Chiefs of Staff Instruction
DoD	U.S. Department of Defense
DoDI	Department of Defense Instruction
IMA	individual mobilization augmentee
JTMD	Joint Table of Mobilization Distribution
MIP	Military Intelligence Program
NIP	National Intelligence Program
PNT	positioning, navigation, and timing
RC	reserve component
RPA	Reserve Personnel Appropriation
SRA	Selected Reserve augmentee
TRMD	trans-regional missile defense
UCP	Unified Command Plan
USSPACECOM	U.S. Space Command

References

Chairman of the Joint Chiefs of Staff Instruction 1001.01C, *Joint Manpower and Personnel Program*, Joint Chiefs of Staff, February 21, 2024.

CJCSI—*See* Chairman of the Joint Chiefs of Staff Instruction.

Department of Defense Instruction 1205.18, *Full-Time Support (FTS) to the Reserve Components*, Office of the Under Secretary of Defense for Personnel and Readiness, June 5, 2020.

Department of Defense Instruction 1215.06, *Uniform Reserve, Training, and Retirement Categories for the Reserve Components*, Under Secretary of Defense for Personnel and Readiness, March 11, 2014, change 2, July 12, 2022.

Department of Defense Instruction 1235.11, *Management of Individual Mobilization Augmentees (IMAs)*, Under Secretary of Defense for Personnel and Readiness, July 10, 2015.

Department of Defense Instruction 3300.05, *Reserve Component Intelligence Enterprise (RCIE) Management*, Under Secretary of Defense for Intelligence and Security, July 17, 2013, change 2, August 7, 2020.

Department of Defense Instruction 3325.11, *Management of the Joint Reserve Intelligence Program (JRIP)*, Under Secretary of Defense for Intelligence and Security, June 26, 2015, change 2, September 24, 2020.

DoDI—*See* Department of Defense Instruction.

Forbes Breaking News, "National Guard and Military Reserve Leaders Testify Before House Appropriations Committee," video, April 30, 2024. As of May 14, 2024:
https://www.youtube.com/watch?v=CRomne-zE98

Joint Chiefs of Staff, "DoD Terminology Program," webpage, undated. As of July 16, 2024:
https://www.jcs.mil/Doctrine/DoD-Terminology-Program/

Joint Chiefs of Staff, *DoD Dictionary of Military and Associated Terms*, April 2024.

MyNavy HR, "Training and Administration of the Reserves (TAR)," webpage, undated. As of March 6, 2024:
https://www.mynavyhr.navy.mil/Career-Management/Detailing/Enlisted/TAR/

Novelly, Thomas, "Space Force Guardians Can Now Choose to Work Part Time Under New Policy Change," military.com, January 18, 2024.

Public Law 113-6, Consolidated and Further Continuing Appropriations Act, 2013; Section 8043, March 26, 2013.

Reserve Forces Policy Board, *Improving the Total Force: Using the National Guard and Reserves*, RFPB Report FY20-01, August 14, 2020.

Taw, Jennifer, and John E. Peters, *Operations Other Than War: Implications for the U.S. Army*, RAND Corporation, MR-566-A, 1995. As of February 15, 2024:
https://www.rand.org/pubs/monograph_reports/MR566.html

U.S. Code, Title 10, Armed Forces; Subtitle E, Reserve Components; Part I, Organization and Administration; Chapter 1005, Elements of Reserve Components; Section 10142, Ready Reserve: Selected Reserve.

U.S. Code, Title 10, Armed Forces; Subtitle E, Reserve Components; Part I, Organization and Administration, Chapter 1007, Administration of Reserve Components; Section 10211, Policies and Regulations: Participation of Reserve Officers in Preparation and Administration.

U.S. Code, Title 10, Armed Forces; Subtitle E, Reserve Components; Part II, Personnel Generally; Chapter 1209, Active Duty; Section 12301, Reserve Components Generally.

U.S. Code, Title 10, Armed Forces; Subtitle E, Reserve Components; Part II, Personnel Generally; Chapter 1209, Active Duty; Section 12302, Ready Reserve.

U.S. Code, Title 10, Armed Forces; Subtitle E, Reserve Components; Part II, Personnel Generally; Chapter 1209, Active Duty; Section 12304, Selected Reserve and Certain Individual Ready Reserve Members; Order to Active Duty Other Than During War or National Emergency.

U.S. Code, Title 10, Armed Forces; Subtitle E, Reserve Components; Part II, Personnel Generally; Chapter 1209, Active Duty; Section 12310, Reserves: For Organizing, Administering, Etc., Reserve Components.

U.S. Code, Title 50, War and National Defense; Chapter 49, Military Selective Service; Section 3819, Authority of President to Order Reserve Components to Active Service; Release from Active Duty; Retention of Unit Organizations and Equipment.

U.S. Department of Defense, *2022 Unified Command Plan*, April 25, 2023, Not available to the general public.

U.S. House of Representatives, Department of Defense Appropriations Act, 2024, Bill 4365, June 27, 2023.

U.S. Space Command, "Frequently Asked Questions," webpage, undated-a. As of November 25, 2024: https://www.spacecom.mil/About/Frequently-Asked-Questions/

U.S. Space Command, homepage, undated-b. As of March 14, 2024: https://www.spacecom.mil/